37 TO ONE

Design: Barbara Poeter Graphic Design, Pittsford, VT

Typesetting: Amy Rothstein, Waltham, MA

Printing: Whitman Communications, Lebanon, NH

Editor: Euan Bear

ISBN: 1-884444-22-9

ORDER FROM:
THE SAFER SOCIETY PRESS
PO Box 340 • Brandon, VT 05733-0340
(802) 247-3132

$12.00
Payable in U.S. funds only
Bulk discounts available

37 to One

LIVING AS AN INTEGRATED MULTIPLE

PHOENIX J. HOCKING

Formerly Sandra J. Hocking

THE SAFER SOCIETY PRESS
PO BOX 340 • BRANDON, VERMONT 05733

DEDICATION

FOR CORA
MY NUMBER ONE FAN
AND FOR FRED

ACKNOWLEDGEMENTS

I WOULD NOT BE whole and inte-grated today without the help and support of my family and friends. I would like to thank them here.

First of all, of course, is Fred, who was midwife at the birth of my whole and integrated self. Many, many thanks. I don't think even today he realizes the difference he made in my life. And for Pam and Bob, who encouraged me to attend massage school in the first place.

Thanks go to my daughter Cora, who, through it all, has stood by me, lis-tened to my rantings and ravings, and loved me anyway.

My husband, Chip, who may not understand it all, but remains the stable rock on which I anchor my life, has earned more than thanks.

Fay Honey Knopp, who encouraged me to submit this manuscript to Safer Society Press. What a good choice, thanks!

Thanks go to Bonnie Denhardt and Eileen Grellert, who read the manu-script and made suggestions that ultimately made the book better.

And last, but certainly not least, thanks to my good friend Linda Badeax Sawyer, who, as usual, helped me push and pull my ramblings into a profes-sional manuscript. I couldn't do any of this without her. And for Drew — thanks for the Chunky Monkey!

CONTENTS

FOREWORD

Once considered a rare psychiatric condition, Multiple Personality Disorder (now known as Dissociative Identity Disorder, or DID) is commonly understood to arise in direct response to severe childhood traumatization and neglect. This shift from rarity to relative commonality during the last 20 years echoes the shift in the understanding of the frequency of physical and sexual child abuse, dissociative responses to trauma, post traumatic stress disorders, and MPD. Of these conditions, MPD has been the most difficult to treat both in its initial stages and through to complete resolution, known as integration of the alternate personalities into one.

Because MPD was considered rare, little information on the dynamics of the disorder and its treatment existed prior to 1980. Since then, however, the professional and self-help literature has blossomed abundantly. Many publications focus primarily on etiological factors (causes), case management, and aspects of treatment. This information has yielded an abundance of books, journals, videos, audiotapes, workshops and conferences on MPD and its treatment from local to international.

Despite this proliferation, however, relatively little is known about successful treatment. Even less is known about the individuals who have achieved integration and what they experienced in the process.

Meeting or even hearing about an integrated multiple is a rare event. Few make themselves publicly known as having once been multiple: it seems to be a secret one keeps about oneself. I'm sure that there are good reasons for that choice (for example, avoiding the freak-show fascination some people show toward multiples). In my travels and communiqués with colleagues and at conferences, the common, softly spoken questions asked (with a wry acknowledgment of the contradictions in terms) is, *Where is everybody? Where are all the integrated Multiples?* Aside from myself, I know of or have met only three others.

Until Phoenix J. Hocking.

In ***37 to One: Living as an Integrated Multiple,*** Phoenix Hocking offers a gift to the professional and lay literature on Multiple Personality Disorder. It is a gift of hope and inspiration to both clients and therapists who work toward resolution of this difficult, complex and bewildering response to profound trauma. Here at last is the first-person account of the final integration of a 37-personality system into one personality. This testimony represents a rare opportunity: even those of us who have worked with multiples rarely hear of successful integrations, and those who integrate seem to disappear into the woodwork of mainstream society, never to be heard of or from again.

Not this time. This time, Phoenix J. Hocking tells us how it went for her before, during and after integration.

She discloses the details of her integration process, reflects on her functioning BI (Before Integration) and AI (After Integration). Phoenix — formerly Sandra J. Hocking, who has written guides for multiples and their families — now shares her experience of integration. And she reminds us that she initially opposed integration of personalities as a treatment goal.

Many multiples fear integration, fearing the "loss" they anticipate to be the inevitable outcome. Phoenix shows us otherwise: "Nothing worth keeping was lost," she writes. It is not the nature of growth, compassion, gratitude, acceptance, and understanding — the core tasks of MPD treatment, alter to alter — to rid itself of itself. Such loss cannot happen, though fear keeps alive the illusion that it will. Over time, through the efforts of therapy and self-scrutiny, change occurs: good change, which ultimately leads to permanent change and the loss of what is no longer needed, the losable. The good remains, to be finessed into everyday life. And that takes time.

Here is information that *integration* is a process, a name for change, and not a "Big Bang Death to Them All." Here is valid testimony that joining (creating cooperation among alternate personalities) can lead to Joining, but that no Joining occurs where guilt, fear, or hatred are present. We learn from Phoenix what integration is and is not, the reality behind the fear. Perhaps the strongest lesson of Phoenix's integration is this: There Is Nothing To Fear.

Phoenix shows us as she learns balance as well as integration, gains insight as well as peace, establishes consistency as well as discovery, and comes into a different level of self-knowledge, born of united consciousness, will and heart. We learn that integration is not a magical transformation into daily bliss, but the amalgamation of all that *was* into daily cohesive function-ing: Being "normal." We learn the vision, perspective, compas-sion, and transcendence of personal history; learn letting it go without bitterness or attachments to past resentments; learn a definition of forgiveness that does not destroy or deny what really happened.

Phoenix's integration, now over 2 years old, stands the test of time. It is proof that integration is possible, achievable, desir-able, and stable.

It is proof that it happens. Here at last is someone else who made it to the end of the course. Those who are running that course now, or who stand on the sidelines coaching the runners should read *37 to One: Living as an Integrated Multiple,* learn its lessons, and be inspired.

Eileen Grellert, Psy.D.

INTRODUCTION ⚏

WHEN I BEGAN to tell people, especially friends who have multiple personalities, that I had integrated, many of the same questions were asked. How had I done it? What does it feel like? Am I lonely? How do I manage life with no help from the alters?

This book, then, is an attempt to share what my journey has been. It is entirely subjective, and in no way should be taken as a road map for your own trek to wellness. We each heal in our own way and in our own time, and no person's travels are exactly like another's.

I suspect that the circumstances of my integration may be unique. The specifics of how and why are not nearly as important as the fact that it happened. And that there *is* life after integration.

I have read numerous stories written by and about people with multiple personalities, and while many are integrated at the end of the book, I had never personally met anyone who had achieved this state of wholeness. It seemed that after integration multiples just fell off the end of the earth and I was always left wondering, "What happens now?" What *is* Sybil doing today? Or Eve?

I imagined that most multiples really remained multiples, and those who integrated did so only in books.

Until it happened to me.

This book, then, is not the story of my life from beginning to end. It is not about all the trials and tribulations that led to my multiplicity and my ultimate integration. It is only the story of one person, one real person, who found integration and healing in a most unexpected place, and what my life is like as a whole person.

This is a small book, a short book. After all, I'm only beginning to set foot on this path of wholeness. You may not find all your answers here, but hopefully, you will find some words of comfort and of hope.

Phoenix J. Hocking
CALIFORNIA

Chapter One

HOW IT HAPPENED

MARCH 26, 1993 — my "birth" date. The location is a school of massage and healing arts in northern California. I have come here to learn to be a massage therapist.

I didn't know I would be born here.

Outside, the day is cool, trees still dripping from a gentle Spring rain. The sweet scent of wood smoke curls up from the chimney, dissipating into a cloudy sky. A large white dog, Star, snoozes on the porch.

Inside the classroom, twelve people struggle with the intricacies of learning massage. Our weeks together have been intense. We have seen each other naked many times, and the novelty has long since worn off. *It's a body; everybody has one; now let's move on.*

For me, it has been a time of wonder, growth, and unexpected joy. Fred, the instructor, has worked as intensely with me as he has with everyone else. He is a gentle soul; quick with laughter, slow to judge, and always, always kind.

We have been learning about the powerful emotions that are often released during massage. I am an incest survivor and a multiple personality, so for me, this is difficult work.

For this session, I am working with Jim.

Jim is tall, muscular, with a gorgeous crop of curly red hair. He is soft spoken and gentle, and gives great hugs. I feel safe with him. Our massage table is set up near the door, away from the radiator, but I am hot and raining sweat anyway.

Jim is working my scapula area, which is tight and tense. I have already had a couple flashbacks of abuse, and I am frightened. I am weeping quietly; I don't even bother to wipe the tears away.

My uncle stands over my crib. I am only six months old. He shoves something in my mouth and I gag. In and out, it is huge, huge. I don't understand, I'm too little to understand. Then something warm and wet is in my mouth, and I start to choke. I am afraid I am going to die. A part of me does die, and another part is born.

I feel Fred's hand on my shoulder. "What's happening?" he asks softly.

The gentleness in his voice breaks through my defenses, and I sob, "I don't know. I just want to curl up and cry."

He assists me and I curl into a ball. Jim continues to work on my back; his hands feel strong, but safe, and I can feel his sweat drip on my body as he works.

"What do you feel?" Fred asks.

"I'm scared!" I cry. Terrified is more like it. Every nerve end is tingling, every hair feels as though it is standing on end in agony.

"Okay, feel it. Feel the fear. Feel *all* the fear."

"I'm afraid I'll switch." I am panicking now. The fear is over-whelming.

"No, you won't."

And he's right. I feel the fear. I let it overtake me, fill me up. I give in to it as completely as if the fear were a lover. Surprisingly, I don't switch. No alter wants this feeling either, and I am stuck with it.

I am three years old. I am floating on the ceiling, somewhere up near the light fixture. Below, some other little girl is being raped. She is screaming, but nobody is home, nobody can hear her. Nobody can help her. I float away, out through the window, into the park. I play with my dollies until it is safe to come back.

Fred continues. He takes me into the fear, through the fear, and out the other side. Miraculously, the fear is gone, and the vision fades.

But there is more. Fred, my instructor and mentor, advances step by step into the muddy battlefield of my soul while Jim massages my body, occasionally murmuring words of encouragement.

Fred pushes, cajoles, urges, helps me to go further than I've ever gone with my therapist. He doesn't let it rest. Inch by inch, we delve into the deepest reaches of my pain. His hands and voice keep me in the present, in this room, in this place.

"What is inside the fear?" he asks.

"Rage!" I cry. And the rage and anger fill me up.

My brother stands before me, hardened penis in his hand, grinning. "Come on," he says, "you know you like it." But I don't like it. I hate it. I hate it! I hate it and I hate him. I am eleven years old.

I shriek, "How could he do that to me? That bastard!!!" I am inside the rage, then through, and out.

"What is inside the rage?"

I look deep inside the anger, and find sadness. Sadness for the little girl abused so long ago. Sadness for the lost years. Sadness for the happy childhood I never had. In, through, out.

"Don't you dare tell Mom."

Inside the sadness is understanding. I see that my brother was acting out his own abuse, also perpetrated by the very uncle who almost choked me to death when I was six months old. I understand that my mother could not acknowledge my abuse without recognizing her own. I know that some members of my family will never quite believe me on this.

Childhood memories file past — Bobby raping me, then me being spanked by Mom for shoving things inside me — Bobby locking me in the toy box — Bobby hitting me, torturing me, until there was no defense but to split into pieces.

I circle and spiral around and around, going deeper and deeper and deeper into my self. Fred holds my hand, his face inches from mine. His breath is warm and sweet against my face. I am both *here*, in the massage room, and *there*, a child again suffering abuse after abuse after abuse. Two places at once.

I feel as though the past and the present are playing a tug-of-war with my soul.

Constantly pushing, Fred gently pulls me farther and farther into and through my pain. Always asking, "What's inside? What is inside this feeling? What is next?" Deeper and deeper, through and out the other side, into the next emotion.

My alters gather around, come in close. I feel their love, and appreciate every one for saving my sanity and my life:

Millie, guardian of the books; Marta, my strong Yorkshire self; Liz, the lesbian, who protects my love of women; Jessica, the virgin teenager; Regina, the whore; Samara, who has no feelings, but records the happenings with no emotion; Misty and Monica, twin children whose only purpose is to play and have fun. Peter, the adventurer and traveler; Danny; The Destroyer; Margret, Betsy, Twelve and Brave, who endured the ritual abuse. Shasha, the little child who cries; Aaron and Rebekah; Jesse; Jeanne and Sandra. The Writer.

Inside the understanding is finally forgiveness. I never expected to forgive my brother for abusing me. I never *wanted* to.

Forgiveness came with understanding the pain of an abused little boy who had nowhere to go with his own rage and pain, and so abused his sister.

So many people to forgive: my uncle and my brother for heaping the most abuse on me; my mother (oh, ouch, and my sainted father, too) for not seeing and stopping the abuse; other family members who just don't believe it ever happened. Myself, for not being strong enough, brave enough, old enough to stop it on my own.

Forgiveness for one means forgiveness for all.

I have gone as far as I can go. I am totally exhausted, and quiet.

But Fred isn't finished with me yet. "What is inside the forgiveness?" he asks.

I can't. Please, I can't go any farther. I can't.

Thirty-seven alters hold their breaths, watching with a mingle of fear, expectation, and hope. Thirty-seven fragments or full-fledged personalities are here to witness my birth.

I don't think there can be anything beyond this, but I look inside anyway. I look, and I see that through all the pain, all the fear, all the abuse, I see the ultimate strength that got me through it all — the inner spirituality that resides in us all, my Higher Power whom I choose to call God.

I breathe out this discovery, tears of joy falling onto the already soaked sheets on the massage table.

"And what is inside God?" he asks.

Inside God? What can possibly be inside God?

I think it is impossible to go any farther. I have seen all there is to see, felt all there is to feel. Know all there is to know.

I reach that last little bit, the one final push into the very center of my being.

Thirty-seven . . .

And inside it all, inside the fear and the rage, the sadness and the understanding, inside the forgiveness and inside even God — I find Peace.

At this moment all the fragments, all my alters, all the scattered and shattered parts of myself embraced, and become one.

I am whole. I am *one.*

★

Chapter Two

HOW IT FEELS

AT FIRST, I didn't trust this feeling. After everything I had read about integration, I knew that this was a very unconventional way to integrate. I doubted it. I tested it at every turn. I put myself into situations that always made me switch previously, and stayed myself.

It's been well over two years now, and the integration is still strong, still holding, still whole. I guess it's real after all.

Like many multiples I know, my alters and I had totally rejected integration as an option. We called it "*the 'I' word,*" and refused to even discuss the possibility with my therapist.

Once, my therapist had attempted an integration of alters, and the result was disastrous. The integration didn't even hold until our next session. The alters were angry because they thought he was trying to "kill" them. We never attempted integration again.

So, how did integration happen without either our conscious consent or desire?

If you read my first book, *Living With Your Selves: A Survival Manual For People With Multiple Personalities*, you may remember my discussing Joining.

Joining is a bit more than cooperation, and a bit less than integration. Joining allows certain alters to come together to complete tasks or handle certain situations, but they are able to separate out again at will.

Just think of a ball of mercury; you can keep it in a little ball, or you can make it into as many separate pieces as you want, then back into a little ball again. Joining is kind of like that.

We had reached the Joining stage some time before. For the most part, except for the most active and strongest, my alters and fragments stayed Joined most of the time.

I had most of my memories, the ones that mattered anyway, so many alters were living in a kind of limbo in which they had nothing to do, no external danger to guard against, and no other alters to protect from internal memories. Everybody knew everybody else and what had happened to them.

When Fred worked with me, I think my alters were ready for integration, even though I don't think *they* knew it.

I had been getting regular weekly massages for about a year before I went to massage school so the alters had already learned that safe touch could feel good. They had learned that both women and men could be trusted. In massage school, the alters learned that the naked body did not have to be a frightening thing.

In fact, we came to enjoy the freedom that comes from being naked in front of others, with no weird sexual energy present — just wearing the suit that God gave us to enjoy the sunshine, the sauna or the hot tub. Massage school was a liberating experience, in more ways than one.

When we reached into that final place, through all the pain and rage, through the tears and found Peace, there was no longer a reason to be separated. Integration was a natural progression in my healing.

I don't want you to think that massage or massage school *caused* my integration, that somehow I went to massage school and *poof!* and *abracadabra!* Fred waved a magic wand and I was integrated. It doesn't happen that way — not by a long shot.

I'd been through, let me see, three, no *four* therapists, only one of whom diagnosed me correctly, off and on over a long period of years. While one ordered group therapy for me, which was helpful, it didn't even touch the underlying reasons for my pain and fear. Another just wanted to prescribe drugs. When just one of the little red pills he ordered for me made me walk around like a zombie all day, I flushed the rest down the toilet.

Another therapist I saw thought all my pain and fear was due to my weight, so I sat in on group therapy for weight loss. I was kicked out of the group because my life story — even without the sexual abuse part of it — was "too hard to compete with" for the other members. It just wasn't a good fit.

After I had my first flashback, I began seeing Bob. Together we finally got to the root of the problems I had been experiencing. We explored the sexual abuse and the ritual abuse. He correctly diagnosed my multiplicity and I got better.

What also helped were all the conferences, workshops and seminars on sexual abuse I was able to attend as a staff member for a women's refuge, an agency working with battered women. These conferences taught me a lot about sexual abuse and survivors. Two psychodrama workshops particularly helped me to believe in my multiplicity: what I saw when I watched myself on the videotape of the session was undeniable. My favorite workshop was the *I Never Told Anyone* workshop led by Ellen Bass and Amy Pine. I felt as though I did years of healing in just one weekend.

I also began an Incest Survivors' Anonymous 12-step peer self-help group and met other Multiples there. Together we began a Multiples group, plus I attended a group specifically for survivors of ritual abuse.

All of these activities helped me to heal and let me be in a receptive place when the right time came. So, you see, I didn't just go to massage school and get "well." We, my alters and I, had worked very hard to get to a place where integration was even possible. We lived with memories and pain and multiplicity. We went to therapy every week for years, cried buckets of tears and screamed shrieks of terror and rage. We had paid our dues. We were ready to move on with life.

So, what's it like, being integrated?

For one thing, every second of every day is mine. I no longer have to share it with others. I no longer have time I can't account for, or clothes I don't remember buying, or speak in voices that don't belong to me.

When I get up in the morning, I know that I am going to be the one to go to bed at night. I can enjoy a movie or a conversation or participate in a class at the college, and know that I will retain the knowledge of all that transpired.

I find that I am blessed with most of the talents and abilities of my alters. I have Marta's strength and thrift (but not her accent); Peter's adventurous spirit (without feeling as though I have to put myself in danger to feel alive); Millie's love of poetry and books (without using literature to hide behind and isolate from others); Liz's forthrightness and love of women (without her lesbian sexual feelings); Shasha's ability to cry (without taking it to extremes); and Misty's capacity for fun (which includes still being silly on occasion).

I didn't lose a thing worth keeping.

I don't hear voices in my head any more. No more conversations inside to keep me awake at night; no more sudden startling shrieks; no more music playing *ad infinitum* in my head, or voices counting out numbers during sex.

Just me, thinking normal thoughts, making decisions, staying present during sex, or arguments, or difficult situations. Just me, enjoying sunsets and music, books and friends.

Just me, figuring out my life and my world on my own.

I expected integration to be sad and lonely and difficult. It has turned out to be none of those things.

I thought I would be lonely, but instead I find that I feel very complete. After all, the alters didn't go anywhere; they're just part of the river of my psyche now, instead of individual streams.

The alters always thought that integration would be like dying. But nobody died! Instead of the alters living *in* me, separately, they now live *as* me, together, if that makes any sense.

We are one person now, not scattered parts. I feel sort of like a jigsaw puzzle, with all the pieces put into place. All the pieces are finally there, and now they fit together to make one whole picture.

When I first started therapy I wanted every memory I had lost. I wanted every single second of my childhood to be restored to me. It was an unrealistic dream. Even singletons can't account for every single second of their childhood. And I can't account for every single second of mine.

Memories are a strange thing anyway. The way I understand it, memories often group together according to similar happenings, so that a person may actually remember as one single incident several different occurrences. So I certainly have enough overview memories to get a pretty clear picture of what happened to me in my past.

The "lost" memories don't matter any more. I have enough memories to know what happened to me without remembering every slap, sexual contact, or ritual.

As Bob, my former therapist, so beautifully put it, "You don't have to count every grain of sand on the beach to know you don't want to build your house there."

I don't need to live on the sand any more, not when solid ground is finally beneath my feet!

I need to make it clear, though, that just because *I* have integrated, and I'm finding integration to be good for *me*, does NOT mean I think *every* multiple ought to integrate. It is certainly okay *not* to choose integration as your final goal.

In my case, the choice to integrate was a subconscious one, and all the circumstances were just right. It happened when we were ready.

Integration, Cooperation, Joining, or remaining a multiple is a decision that needs to be reached within your own individual systems (consciously or subconsciously), with the help of your therapist. What is good for me may not be right for you; only you can make the decision what to do with your life.

Chapter Three

NAMING MY WHOLE SELF

O TELL YOU the truth, the decision to change my name was absolutely spur-of-the-moment. We were standing in a circle that last day of massage school, saying good-bye, and I was so overcome with how different I felt, that I announced I was going to change my name. I don't know how many multiples change their names upon integration, but for me, it just seemed right. Somehow, *Sandra*, with all the emotional baggage that went along with that name, just did not fit any more.

It is a six-hour drive from the massage school to the small northern California town where I live. I left massage school late in the afternoon; it was cool and overcast. The winding mountain road from the coast demanded much of my attention, but my mind was on changing my name.

Stopping for the night, I treated myself to a nice dinner, then went to a nice motel. The television sitcoms were dull and boring. I didn't feel like reading. I felt drained and tired, so I went to sleep early.

That night, I dreamed of a beautiful bird, rising from ashes and flames, and soaring into a clear blue sky. I dreamed of freedom.

The next day, continuing the drive home, the name change nagged at me. I tried to talk myself out of it. I told myself that changing my name at this stage of my life was ridiculous, that it would involve all sorts of paperwork and money, that it would probably be more trouble than it would be worth.

But in the end, I knew it was right for me after all.

The first thing I did when I got home was tell my husband that I was going to change my name. Then, I called Fred at the school and asked him to put my massage therapy certificate in my new name — Phoenix Jeanne Hocking.

I decided on the name *Phoenix*, partly because of my dream from the night before, and partly because it just seemed right. Rising from the scattered ashes of a shattered past, to emerge whole and gleaming into the sunlight that almost destroyed it — terribly apropos, don't you think?

I kept my middle name, though. Somehow it did not seem right to throw *everything* away. After all, I had turned out to be a pretty decent human being, and I wanted to honor those in my childhood that had made that possible. *Jeanne* holds no emotional baggage for me.

I soon found that changing my name was both easy and difficult. After all, I'd been Sandra for 44 years. Everyone knew me as Sandra; all my legal papers were in that name. My previous two books are written under that name.

But I also knew that the name Sandra just didn't fit any more, and Phoenix did. I felt as though I had outgrown *Sandra*, and was ready to grow up and be an adult.

So I went to court and had my name changed. I have included the particulars in an appendix to this book, if you're at all interested in the procedure.

If you should decide to change your own name at integration, don't expect fireworks and roses. Changing my name took less than one minute in front of the judge.

Recognizing that free advice is usually worth exactly what you pay for it, may I give just a little suggestion here anyway? If you change your name, have a party! Invite your friends over, decorate the house, serve cheeseburgers and hot fudge sundaes and sparkling cider. Have a ceremony that will be meaningful to you. Throw everything you possess with your old name on it into a huge bonfire, and kiss that part of your life good-bye!

I didn't, and now I wish I had.

The legal stuff was easy. It was far more difficult to get my friends and family to start using my new name. Heck, I have friends who never made the change from Sandy to Sandra, so changing to Phoenix was like trying to pull hen's teeth with a pair of pliers. One of my brothers even refused to use my new name until I sent him a copy of the legal court documents!

When people still call me *Sandra*, I often just smile and say, "Sandra doesn't live here any more!" Eventually they catch on.

Sometimes, though, I still use my old name when I talk to myself. If I do something dumb, I'm more likely to go "Oh, Sandra, you dummy, whadja do that for?" than "Oh, Phoenix, you made a mistake!"

Oh well, some things just take time, I guess.

★

Chapter Four

MAKING PEACE
WITH MY PAST

INTEGRATION DOES NOT mean that my past just went away. Nothing can change what happened to me.

I am aware of some therapies that call for the survivor to change the outcome of their abuse in their heads, but that has never made much sense to me. What happened, happened. It's not truthful or beneficial for me to change the outcome in my mind. I have to accept everything that happened, make peace with it, and move on.

Name it, claim it, and let it go.

For most of my life, I lived in a reactive state, seeing life through the smoky haze of past hurts and abuses. I couldn't quite distinguish between what was happening *now* and what happened *then*.

The memories I have of my past are a hodge-podge of pain and pleasure. On one end I remember times of great joy, often with my father, before he passed away. I remember sitting on the window seat, listening to Daddy taping stories on an old reel-to-reel tape recorder, sometimes having to pause to allow the trucks to pass by on the freeway.

I remember playing "tickle backs" with my sister, an early foray into my current massage therapy. We would rub each others backs, usually for one song or two on the radio, then switch, before finally drifting off to sleep.

I remember getting up before dawn and accompanying my father down to the breakwater, where we kids would catch small fish in the harbor, which he would then use as bait to catch the larger ocean fish.

And I remember, early, early on, my first attempts at writing poetry, and how much praise was heaped upon me for being so clever.

Yet, in with the "good" memories are plenty of bad ones. Being abused, feeling outraged at the abuse, yet powerless to stop it.

Satanic rituals with the neighbors next door. Being forced to engage in bestiality, cannibalism, or watch ritual murder.

Being beaten, raped, tied up, locked in a closet.

Getting hit in the eye with a mud ball. My father's death and funeral.

All this pain was too overwhelming for such a little girl to handle. The good and pleasant happenings in my life were no match for the horror of the bad experiences.

Multiplicity allowed me to keep the good memories and make them my own, while, at the same time, take the bad memories and incidents and partition them off into the alters.

I don't know what caused my uncle to become a child molester. I know some pieces of family history that indicate he may have been abused himself at some point in his life. He in turn, abused my brother, who abused me. It was a horrible cycle that, thank God, broke with me.

Back forty and fifty years ago, when my brother and I were being sexually and ritually abused, child abuse was just not talked about. Children who were abused had no way to express their pain. Such abuse was hidden away, suffered in silence, and on the rare occasions it was discovered, it was brushed under the carpet and never mentioned again.

In such an atmosphere of denial and fear, where could a boy child (my brother) go with that kind of rage, that kind of pain? How could he possibly grow up strong and healthy and loving with such a horrible secret in his past? A secret nobody ever talked about, nobody ever let him cry over, nobody ever told him wasn't his fault?

What about my parents? Why didn't they see and stop what was happening? I'm convinced that my mother was abused by her brother (my uncle). Although she denies it and will never admit such a thing, she bears many signs of being a sexual abuse survivor. If my assumption is true, it makes sense that she couldn't allow herself to see and acknowledge my abuse without recognizing her own. And she can't do that, for whatever reason.

Besides, I went to great lengths to hide my abuse from my family. I created other personalities to live life with a smile. How could my parents possibly have known when I made damn sure they never found out?!

My father was a dreamer. He saw the best in people all the time. There was no capacity for evil within him, and he couldn't recognize it in others. So when the ultimate evil was happening right underneath his very nose, he didn't see it. People simply didn't do such things to others, so the abuse happening in his own house just didn't exist.

Because I was abused so young, I found trusting difficult.

Yet I wanted so desperately to believe that people *could* be trusted I sometimes went one hundred and eighty degrees in the opposite direction and trusted *everybody*, even those who were obviously untrustworthy.

Since integration, I find that I can more accurately judge who can be trusted and who can't. I have grown beyond my child-hood inability to see people as they really are, and have a better grasp for those who do not have my best interests at heart. I have learned to be optimistically cautious in my dealings with people.

Integration means that I have had to accept *all* the memories of the alters and of myself, as my own. Everything that happened to *them*, happened to *me*. And everything *they* did, *I* did.

Part of making peace with my past means forgiving those who abused me, those who didn't (or couldn't) protect me, and those who did not or do not believe me.

As I said before, I certainly never expected or wanted to forgive anybody. And I don't necessarily advocate forgiveness as something everyone must do in order to heal. For me, it just happened.

Forgiveness doesn't mean saying that what was done to me was okay. It wasn't. The abuse hurt me — it almost destroyed my life. It split my psyche into 37 different pieces and twisted my view of the world. No, what happened to me was definitely *not* okay.

For me, forgiveness means not carrying around the burden of blame any more. If blame means to hold someone else at fault for everything that happens in my life, then I could easily have gone on living that way. But that doesn't work for me today. Today I have to take responsibility for my own actions.

Hating and blaming my abusers didn't hurt *them*; it only hurt *me*. My abusers are either dead, injured beyond help, or members of a satanic coven* that I wouldn't recognize if I passed them on the street today. Hating them only ate into my own soul, and buried the burgeoning feelings of love and joy in my life.

Blaming my abusers became too heavy a burden; it took too much energy, too much time, too much away from me. Blame only bound me closer to my abusers instead of relegating them to the past where they belonged.

Covens are groups of people who meet together to practice religious rituals. Some are positive and connect with nature. But in *my* history, a coven was a gathering of satanists who believed in the devil and practiced sexual abuse as part of their rituals.

Condemning myself, for being small, for being weak, for not being able to stop the abuse, and for certain behaviors that some alters engaged in, tore tiny chunks out of my self-esteem every day. Finally, I realized that it wasn't worth it to me to hold on to these feelings.

I had a lot of people to forgive, too. My uncle for starting (or continuing?) the cycle of abuse in my family; my brother for heaping the most abuse on me; my parents for not seeing and stopping the abuse; other family members who just don't believe the abuse ever happened. I also had to forgive myself for the sometimes inappropriate or destructive actions of my alters.

Besides forgiving my brother, I feel pity for him now, and see him as yet another victim of child abuse; a victim who never got help, and so acted out his rage and pain on me, his younger sister. The sad part is that he will never be able to get help. Some years ago, he was in a car accident that pretty much scrambled his brains. There isn't enough left of him to heal. He spends his life in a nursing home, unable to work, read, or hold a coherent thought or memory for more than a minute. Even if he remembers his own abuse, or mine, the capacity for remorse and healing no longer exists.

Yet, within the forgiveness and the pity, there is also relief that he is in a position where he no longer has access to children, and can't hurt anybody else any more.

For me, forgiving one means forgiveness for all. Forgiveness, to me, means no longer focusing on the harm that was done to me through the abuse, but being thankful for the strength I gained from surviving it. It means being grateful that I have used the experiences of my past to help others. Because of my own abuse, I am able to be compassionate and caring toward others in pain.

The great philosopher Nietzsche once said, "that which does not kill me makes me stronger." The abuse shattered me and forced my psyche into 37 different pieces, but it didn't kill me. And I think I am stronger in the broken places that have healed than I might have been otherwise.

Chapter Five

CHANGING MY LIFE

O F COURSE MY life changed after integration. All of a sudden, I had all this time to myself. Every minute of every day, remember? It isn't always easy. But, it isn't always difficult, either.

Before integration, I had stopped working because the stress of my job with a women's refuge was more than I could take at the time. I could never be sure what would trigger a switch or a flashback. I was terrified that an alter would emerge at work, and say or do something inappropriate. I was never quite sure of myself, even though my co-workers had no idea of the pain I was going through.

After I integrated, my expectations of myself went up. I now no longer have the excuse of multiplicity for not accomplishing my goals. I can't blame my eccentricities on my alters; I have to claim them as my own. And when I get tired, I can't just switch into an alter with more energy to get the job done. I've had to learn how to rest, how to pace myself, and how to say "no" when some request will result in an overload.

I'm learning to say, "I'll think about it and get back to you," when asked to do something. In my multiple days, I said "yes" to just about anything, knowing that if I couldn't handle it, there was always an alter who could take over. Now, I'm more aware of my own limitations of time and energy.

I'm also learning how to solve problems on my own, without all that internal input I was used to. I don't have "The Committee" debating every decision in my head any more. It feels wonderful to know that I am capable of taking care of my own problems.

Integration means not only accepting the wonderful traits of my alters as my own, it also means having to accept the less than wonderful traits, too.

For example, feeling anger was something The Destroyer did; now I get to feel it. I am still learning to identify when some happenstance is truly worthy of my anger, or if I'm simply reacting to old tapes. I've had to learn to channel justifiable anger in appropriate and assertive ways. No longer can I beat the shinola out of the hearth with a piece of firewood. I have to speak up and not allow myself to be walked on, but I can't be violent to myself or others.

Sadness belonged to Shasha. For Shasha, because she was a child, it was okay to curl up into a little ball and sob for hours and not accept any help. Sadness is okay. Crying is okay. But not accepting help, comfort and support from those who care about me is *not* okay for me any longer.

Sex was Regina's. I have to be totally honest here, because I don't want to give you the impression that integration means *all* my troubles are over. Sex is still a problem for me. Regina's original name was "The Whore." She was promiscuous, if not in deed, certainly in thought and in word.

During the time that I was healing, my husband generously agreed to a sexless life (mostly because Regina felt she wasn't married to him, and nobody else in the system, including me, wanted to have sex with anybody).

Luckily, I'm married to a man with infinite patience. He is willing to help me work on this last bit of healing that I still need to do, whether that means remaining celibate for long periods of time, or having sex that is less than satisfactory. I'm a lucky woman to have such a man in my life.

One of the most difficult things for me to accept was that everything an alter did, *I* did. The alters were not created out of nothing, so I must accept that within me all along was the capacity to feel the things the alters felt, and to do the things the alters did.

This was a hard truth for me to swallow. Some of my alters engaged in behaviors I find repugnant, disgusting and shameful. It hurts to think that I have the potential for such behavior within me. And yet, if I didn't have it somewhere within my soul, my alters would not have had it either.

Before integration, I would answer the question, "How much of them is you?" with the answer, "Well, anger belongs to The Destroyer, sex belongs to Regina," and so forth. Today, difficult as it sometimes is to accept, I would have to answer, "They are *all* me."

Before integration, I was often stuck in depression until switching to a different alter got me out of it. Now, if I'm sad, I cry. But I also let people who love me give me a hug, and I'm able to tell myself that "this, too, shall pass." I'm able to pick myself up, dust myself off, and go on with life.

It takes some time and practice to feel emotions responsibly. I make mistakes; I'm still learning how to express my emotions in a manner that is healthy for me, and not destructive to others.

Sometimes I miss having the alters to talk to. And sometimes I miss being able to blurt out whatever I'm thinking and expect that people will just blame my words on an alter.

And sometimes, I even miss the excitement of being a multiple. Let's face it, when you're a multiple there is always something new to work on, or some alter's behavior to clean up after, or even the attention that comes with the label of multiplicity. I miss that, sometimes. But I find that I miss it less and less the longer I remain integrated.

Being a multiple is like being part of an exclusive club, a club where everybody understands you, and a certain bond holds you all close to each other. Now, when I'm around my friends who are multiples, I sometimes feel a little left out.

For me, though, I'm finding that integration is so much better than being multiple. The joy that I feel each morning when I get up and know that I haven't lost a day or two is indescribable. Being able to go to work, and know that I can do my job *myself* has certainly raised my self-esteem.

Just being able to stay present in difficult situations has been growth for me. Learning a task and retaining the knowledge is wonderful.

Mostly, though, for me, integration means freedom. Freedom to live *my* life in any way I see fit. It means the freedom to choose my companions, my jobs, my activities, and my beliefs. Integration means relieving myself of the horrible burden of identifying myself as a "victim," in all phases of my life.

I'm not a victim any more. And "survivor" is only *one* label I use to describe myself, not the *only* one.

Chapter Six

BEING PRESENT

A FEW DAYS ago, I bought a hat. There is nothing particularly earthshaking about that except that I've never worn hats — Marta did. Hats always looked strange on me, like they didn't quite belong. But I saw this great white cloche in a thrift store for three bucks, tried it on, and loved it. Marta would have approved, I think.

I said earlier that when I integrated I didn't lose a thing worth keeping, and that's true, for the most part. Just as I now own adult coloring books and colored pens instead of Mickey Mouse and crayons, this hat represents the part of Marta that is me.

The other day I tried to speak in Marta's broad Yorkshire accent…and couldn't. The accent just wouldn't come. Did I lose the accent when I integrated? Marta always said that the accent was simply an affectation she used so that I would know that it was she speaking. If the accent didn't really belong to her, then it didn't really belong to me, either.

Peter was the adventurer in my internal system. He thought it necessary to put us into danger by taking us to the "bad" parts of town, or standing in front of open windows half-clothed, or engaging in other behaviors that were in some way dangerous. Now, that adventurous and education-seeking spirit finds release in taking classes at the college, or going on trips that involve hiking or other physical activities.

Millie's love of books and poetry were easy to assimilate, as were the sense of fun and games of Misty and Monica. Just as Millie would spend hours at a library, and loved to curl up with a good book on a cold winter's night, so do I. Laughter and joy and sometimes being silly are a part of my everyday existence, not isolated incidents limited to when the twins were expressing themselves outwardly. Such behaviors and parts of my personality are easy to acknowledge and enjoy.

But the attributes of some of the alters have not been as easily accepted.

Liz, for example, was a non-practicing lesbian. How does that apply to me, a married woman? In theory, you would think that I would be sexually attracted to women, but the reality is that what Liz saw as sexuality, I have translated into finally being able to be friends with women. The fact that Liz never acted out her sexual feelings towards women made it easier for me.

The Destroyer was angry all the time. He beat on things until he broke them. He injured the body by cutting, scraping, or pulling hair. When I integrated, I was most afraid of how all this anger and pain would make the transition. I was afraid that I would not be able to control my anger.

To my surprise, I found that anger is just an emotion. It does not have a life of its own unless I allow it to. When I'm angry, I stop, take a deep breath, count alligators if I have to, then try to talk it out with the source of my anger, if possible. The anger is no longer rage; it is a controllable emotion for me today.

In the present, I am able to take the abilities, talents and attributes of my alters and keep what is worth keeping. I can replace behaviors and thoughts I consider less desirable with others I deem more acceptable to me. Today, I have the *choice* of how I live my life.

When I think about it, the freedom to choose how I live my life is the greatest gift of all.

Take working, for example. Throughout much of my therapy, I was working full-time at a women's refuge, sometimes 60 or 80 hours a week, with energy to spare. If I got tired, or stressed out, or overworked, there was always an alter available to take over. If I didn't know how to help a particular client, Roberta usually knew just the right thing to say. Or if I got stage-fright speaking in front of a room full of cops or therapists, Kate just stepped to the forefront and completed the speech.

Now, I have to pace myself. I can't work a hundred hours a week and expect not to get tired. Being whole means learning to take care of myself, not overdo, not overextend myself. But being whole also means I can give myself permission to *be* tired, that it's okay to accept the limitations of my body and my stamina.

It also means watching what comes out of my mouth! I have to take responsibility for the words I speak. I can't blame a social *faux pas* on an alter. And if I do say something inappropriate, rude or insensitive, then I feel obliged to make amends immediately.

I think the most difficult part for me is learning to be assertive. I had alters who were aggressive, alters who were regressive, and alters who were downright bullies. Liz and Marta were both assertive, so at least I have something to build on. Being assertive gets easier all the time.

Being assertive means standing up for myself without stepping all over the feelings of others. It means speaking in terms of "I." Not, "*you* made me feel this way," but "*I* feel this way." It means owning my feelings, and expressing them in a manner that does not offend others (or myself).

Being assertive means taking care of myself first, before I try to save the world. Yes, I admit it. One of the many things that has survived integration is my feeling that I need to be of some service in this world. That's not necessarily a bad thing. In fact, it's one of the things I like best about myself.

I used to be terrific at telling other people how to take care of themselves. In fact, if you've read my first two books, you'll see entire chapters on how to take care of yourself. But the truth is, I was *terrible* at following my own advice!

Now, I go to bed at ten o'clock at night instead of staying up until two or three in the morning to write. I take bubble baths, listen to soft music, and go for walks with my dogs. Reading and writing poetry, snuggling up with an Agatha Christie novel in front of the fire, getting hugs from people I care about — all the activities I recommended to others are ones I now do for myself.

You know something? I give pretty good advice! This stuff feels great!!

Chapter Seven

GETTING THROUGH THE ROUGH SPOTS

I DON'T WANT you to think that when I integrated all my problems disappeared. They didn't. It would be nice if life were a Disney movie, where the boy gets the girl, or the dogs arrive home safely, or the lion claims his rightful heritage and everybody lives happily ever after.

You and I both know life isn't like that.

About a year into integration, I hit a major rough spot. My life was fine, but I wasn't. I was bored, restless, and depressed. I missed the excitement of being a multiple, I missed therapy, I missed the roller-coaster ride of emotions to which I had become accustomed.

I had become addicted to "new," to change, to excitement, and the same old solid, stable life was boring me to tears.

I contemplated moving to Maine and building a cabin in the woods. I thought about going to school and learning yet another trade. I went back to work part-time, even though my husband and I are both "retired." I felt something major was missing in my life.

I was spending my days in front of the television watching soap operas, and my nights in front of the television stuffing my face with ice cream, cookies and pretzels.

What the heck was wrong with me?

You may remember from my first book, *Living With Your Selves*, that I had my first memory of childhood abuse after I had been abstinent from compulsive eating for two years.* I had lost a lot of weight, my life was great, and then the memories began. The alters activated and I was thrown into the pit of multiplicity, memories, denial, and pain.

During my recovery I'd gained back the seventy or so pounds I had lost when I was not overeating. I dumped the emotional baggage, only to discover that the physical baggage was back, with a vengeance.

I realized that I was afraid. Afraid that if I lost weight, if I again became abstinent from compulsive eating, it would start all over — all the pain, all the memories, all the rage, (maybe even the multiplicity) — and I'd be right back where I started. The very thought terrified me.

---

*This is a 12-step phrase from Overeaters Anonymous that means I wasn't compulsively eating. I can't say I "got control over" my compulsive eating, because wanting or trying to *control* things sinks me every time. It's not quite like "giving up" a behavior, because being abstinent means making conscious, active choices every day, not only *not* to do whatever it is, but *to* do something more constructive instead.

But I've had to face the fact that some problems I had when I started this pilgrimage are still here. The difference is that now the problems are all mine.

But if the problems are mine, then so are the solutions. Now, I have the strength to recognize both, and the courage to put the solutions to work in my life.

I am solely responsible for what goes into my mouth, for example. I can't blame my weight on an alter who sabotages my diet. I have to take responsibility for the foods I eat, both healthy and destructive. I have to take responsibility for the exercise I get, or don't get, as the case may be.

Learning to overcome these fears is a slow, daily process. It doesn't happen overnight. And I can't do it alone. Every day I get support from my husband, my family, and my friends. Every day I turn to the spirituality of my life to help me sort out the bad times, and the good.

I didn't "get religion." I didn't become a Bible thumper; I didn't turn New Age or Buddhist or any particular religion. I only found the spirituality that had been within me all along.

I know that for many of you, any discussion of a Higher Power, God or spirituality or whatever you want to call it in any form may be distressing. I understand. I was abused during religious rituals, and I know how cunning and powerful those old memories and lessons can be.

But my story would not be complete without saying that I believe it was this innate sense of spirituality that helped me live my life, even through the abuse, the memories and even integration.

I choose to call this sense of spirituality God. You can call it whatever you want, of course, but it is this profound belief, this sense of being cared for and loved, no matter what, that gets me through my days.

When I was being ritually abused, the one thing the members of the coven tried to take away from me was my spirituality, and replace it with theirs. But they couldn't. I kept the God of my understanding, who is kind, loving, and gentle, deep within my heart, even as they abused my body. I hung on to the belief that my God was stronger than their Satan. My God loves me just as I am, and loves everybody else too (even my abusers), regardless of race, creed, color, religion or anything else. It is this spirituality that sustains me today.

One of the problems that still remains is that of my weight. Left to my own devices, I would eat myself into an early grave. I have no willpower when it comes to food, which I often call my "drug of choice." But I'm working on it, and even when I falter, I know that I still have the capability to win even this battle. After all, if I can heal from sexual abuse, I can certainly heal from compulsive eating. It just takes time.

I'm still fundamentally a restless person. I used to think that I was restless because I had so many different parts of me that wanted to do different things. But since I've integrated, I find that I'm still restless. I get bored easily, especially if I'm doing a job that I already know how to do. I enjoy learning new things, having new experiences, and traveling whenever possible to new and exciting places. I am my father's daughter, after all, and we were both born with itchy feet. It seems the grass is *always* greener somewhere else.

I would like to say that all the doubts and fears I had during my childhood and throughout my therapy went away when I integrated. But they didn't.

I still sometimes wonder if I made it all up.

I still sometimes wonder if I was ever really a multiple at all.

I still sometimes wonder if this is just a brief respite, and that maybe the multiplicity will return if I delve too deeply into the issues still remaining. I wonder if the alters are just taking a vacation, or if I'm deluding myself into believing that I've integrated.

Ninety-nine-point-nine percent of the time, though, I know my truth is real, that I was abused, that I was indeed a multiple, and that I truly have integrated. When doubt and fear have been a determining factor in 40-odd years of life, it is sometimes difficult to make changes and push those doubts and fears away.

Difficult, but not impossible.

I have to admit to myself that I am powerless over food, my life and my past. I can't change or fix what happened to me.

Being powerless, however, is not the same thing as being helpless. I am not helpless. Today, for example, I have the choice of what food goes into my mouth. I can decide not to let the experiences of my past ruin my present and my future. I can choose to do the things that are good for my health and my body and my soul.

So, as you can see, I still have lots to work on. Life, after all, is never a flat line, but a series of peaks and valleys. I am buoyed by my friends and family; I am sustained by my spirituality; I am free to choose, free to solve problems, free to enjoy life. So, what's a few problems? I can handle them now.

★

Chapter Eight

WHAT NOW?

I'VE BEEN INTEGRATED now for well over two years. I have to admit that I wondered many times if this was real. I had heard about people having brief "flights into health," and I wondered if that was what happened to me. But, my goodness, two years is an awfully long flight, if that be true. So, I can only assume that, by golly, I really have integrated, and my life is better in many respects than I ever imagined life could be.

Gone are the nightmares that visited me three or four or five times a night. Gone are the irrational fears of people, places and things that terrorized my days. Gone is that feeling of having no control over my own life.

Now, I sleep through the night. I have choices in how I live my life, what people I associate with, what food I eat, what activities I engage in.

I have more time than I know what to do with. When I had to share time with 37 alters, I had little time to myself. Now, I have 24 entire hours a day to fill with activities I enjoy.

How *do* I spend my life now?

A typical day looks something like this:

I get up about 5:30 every morning to let the dogs out. Then I go back to bed for an hour or so. I start the day with a prayer and a shower (usually in that order). I go downstairs, fix the coffee and feed the dogs and cats (four dogs, three cats). A bite of breakfast, then off to the den, where I write.

I try to write for a couple of hours every day. In addition to this book, I'm also working on a couple of children's books, some short stories, and have a list of self-help books that I plan to write.

Sometimes I go out and help my husband in the yard. We're building a fence in the back yard so the dogs can have more space to run. It's backbreaking, hard, physical labor, and I'm sore afterwards, but it feels good to be accomplishing something useful. Later, my friend Sydney has promised to help me learn how to plant a vegetable and flower garden.

I don't watch the soaps any more. Occasionally, I'll check in to see what's happening on *General Hospital* and *Days of Our Lives*, but for the most part, the television doesn't come on until evening.

I clean the house, do the laundry, wash the dishes — you know, housework (which I still hate, by the way!).

I'm working as a clerk at a pharmacy. It's rewarding, interesting work that adds a couple pennies to the budget and keeps me busy besides. I like working there. My co-workers know about my past, and are supportive.

I like working with the public, and bend over backwards to be as cheerful and helpful as I can be. I figure, if a person is picking up a prescription, it's because either they don't feel good, somebody they care about doesn't feel good, or they need this medication to stay alive. That's plenty of reason to be nice to people, as far as I'm concerned. I'm nice to them, and they're nice to me. It's a great arrangement!

Evenings are spent fixing and cleaning up after dinner, watching a little television, playing cards or Scrabble, or putting together a jigsaw puzzle with my husband.

Sometimes we go camping, or traveling, or just out for a walk, enjoying the fresh air.

Whenever I am asked to speak at child-abuse conferences, I'm always happy to do so. My boss is generously flexible regarding my public-speaking engagements. Speaking at conferences is just one of the ways I try to help.

Last winter I started The Sleeping Bag Project, an organization that collects donations and distributes clothing and other items to homeless people.

I try to attend a support group for overeaters about twice a week. After all, now that the emotional baggage is mostly gone, the physical baggage has got to go, too. Without the support these meetings provide, my life, integrated or not, would probably be a shambles today. They have been a life-saver for me.

Mostly, my life is what I consider "normal." I laugh a lot now and am able to see the humor in life. I love to bake bread from scratch, write long letters, play chess and read. I love waking up in the morning with one little dog curled up at my chest and another at my feet.

I have goals now. I plan to write an entire series of books. I plan to someday own a bookstore and tea shop in Vermont. I plan to finally drop this excess weight and learn to enjoy exercising. I plan to take a trip to Europe with my husband.

I plan to live every minute God gives me with joy. The wonderful thing is, now that I have integrated, I can look forward to actually achieving my goals.

Egad! How normal, how boring, how ... wonderful! To have a normal life, whole days in which I get to live my own life — what a gift, what a joy!

As I said in the beginning, this book is only about my own experiences as a whole and integrated person. I don't know how my experiences correspond with those of other integrated multiples. I only know that for me, life is better than I ever thought it could be.

From my point of view, the problems aren't all gone, but now I am able to deal with them much better than when I was split into pieces.

Integration is not death. Integration has turned out to be the gift of life for me, and I'm glad it happened.

If you make a conscious or subconscious decision that integration is for you, I just want you to know that there is, indeed, life after integration. And while Sandra may not live here any more, Phoenix is alive and living well.

★

THE END
(Of the Beginning)

NAME CHANGING: THE PROCESS

I DON'T KNOW how many multiples change their names when they integrate, or for that matter, how many survivors do during their healing, but for me it was the right thing to do. It occurred to me that some people might be interested in the process, so I have included it here:

The first thing I did was go to the bookstore and get a copy of *How To Change Your Name*, by David Ventura Loeb and David Brown. In this wonderful book I found all the information I needed for changing my name. (I live in California, so bear in mind that regulations for changing one's name may vary from state to state.)

One method for changing your name is called the Usage Method, which basically means that you simply start using your new name in all your personal and business affairs. And in the beginning, that's just what I did. I wrote a letter saying that I had changed my name from *Sandra Jeanne Hocking* to *Phoenix Jeanne Hocking*, had it notarized, and sent copies to family, friends, colleagues, and everybody with whom I did business. Bingo, one changed name.

Now, the Usage Method is perfectly legal, but the Court Method is necessary for a passport until you've been using your new name for at least five years. And, as my husband and I were planning a trip to Europe (we're *always* planning a trip to Europe — we haven't gotten there yet!), I needed to go to court to have my name changed.

Going to court involved typing up the appropriate *In Pro Per* papers (some states may require a lawyer), paying the fee, advertising my name change in the newspaper for four weeks, and showing up in court on the appointed day. Lots of paperwork, but nothing too complicated.

It was July 6th, just after Independence Day (again, quite appropriate). Hot, but not muggy; crystal clear blue skies, birds singing in the trees. And, boy, was I was nervous!

I went alone. As much as I would have liked my husband to join me, I felt that this was something I needed to do by myself.

I had no idea what to expect. I sat through various other civil cases, listening and wondering when my turn would come.

The clerk finally called my name: "Sandra Jeanne Hocking."

I stood up, came forward, and said, "That's me."

Judge: "This petition is for a change of name. No opposition has been filed. I see no opposition. Petition granted."

Me: "Thank you, your honor."

And that was it.

I was legally and officially *Phoenix Jeanne Hocking,* an integrated, whole and self-named person.

In a few weeks, I received two legal copies of the document changing my name, one from the courts and the other from the state of California. Some people may wish to send a copy to the town clerk in the town where they were born to request an amended birth certificate. I chose not to, mostly because I thought it might create problems for descendants doing genealogical research later.

So, after all this, getting a new passport was no problem! I simply sent a certified copy of my change of name along with my old passport to the nearest passport office. They made the change and sent it back to me. Easy as pie.

SELECTED RESOURCES ON MULTIPLICITY AND HEALING

THE FOLLOWING BOOKS and publications are ones that I found helpful. Many are survivor's stories. Some may be out of print or no longer stocked in bookstores, but you may be able to find them in libraries or through out-of-print book search services. Beyond the books and publications, you'll find a brief resource list of helpful organizations and catalogs.

BOOKS

Living With Your Selves: A Survival Manual For People With Multiple Personalities by Sandra J. Hocking (yes, that's me!). 1992. $7.00. Available from your bookstore, or direct from the publisher, Launch Press. Call 1-800-321-9167.

Someone I Know Has Multiple Personalities: A Book For Significant Others: Family, Friends and Caring Professionals by Sandra J. Hocking. 1994. $7.00. Available from your bookstore, or direct from Launch Press.

The Hope of Recovery: A Message of Hope and Encouragement for Multiple Personality Clients and Those Who Treat Them (Video: 59 minutes.) Features a discussion among three women in various stages of recovery and integration (including Eileen Grellert, who wrote the Foreword to this book!). Available from Varied Directions International: call Joyce at 1-800-888-5236 (ask about the discount price for MPD/DID clients).

Reach for the Rainbow: Advanced Healing for Survivors of Sexual Abuse by Lynne D. Finney, J.D., M.S.W. 1992. $12.95. Putnam Publishing Group. Available from your bookstore.

Unchained Memories: True Stories of Traumatic Memories, Lost and Found by Lenore Terr, M.D. 1994. $12.95. Basic Books. Available from your bookstore.

Sybil by Flora Schreiber. The classic. 1989. $5.95 Warner Books.

When Rabbit Howls by The Troops for Truddi Chase. This is available in both hardback and paperback. 1990. $5.99 (paper). Jove Publications.

United We Stand by Eliana Gil, Ph.D. 1990. $5.95. Launch Press. Written in an easy-to-understand style, Dr. Gil explains multiplicity to multiples and non-multiples alike.

Suffer The Child by Judith Spencer. 1989. $4.99. Paperback Books. Ritual abuse, graphic. Not for the faint-hearted.

Katherine, It's Time by Kit Castle and Stefan Bechtel. 1990. $5.99. Avon Books.

Voices by Trula LaCalle (apparently out of print, but possibly traceable).

The Minds of Billy Milligan by Daniel Keyes. 1982. $4.50. Bantam Books.

My Father's House by Sylvia Fraser. 1989. $11.00. Harper Collins.

Ghost Girl by Torey Hayden. 1992. $4.99. Avon Books.

Diagnosis and Treatment of Multiple Personality Disorder by Dr. Frank Putnam. 1989. $38.95. Guilford Press. Clinical literature, but very readable.

MPD From The Inside Out edited by Barry M. Cohen, Esther Giller, and Lynn W. 1991. $14.95. Sidran Press. Submissions by many multiples from all over the country.

Mending Ourselves expressions of healing and self-integration by the readers of *Many Voices*. 1993. $12.95. Many Voices Press.

Multiple Personality Disorder (MPD) Explained For Kids by Gary Peterson, MD, and Barbara W. Boat, PhD. 1991. $4.00 University of North Carolina, Chapel Hill, NC (phone 1-919-966-1760).

The Flock by Joan Casey. 1991. $23.00. Knopf.

NEWSLETTERS AND SURVIVORS' PUBLICATIONS

Many Voices PO Box 2639, Cincinnati, OH 45201-2639.

Moving Forward PO Box 4426, Arlington, VA 22204 / phone: 703-271-4024. Bimonthly newsletter "for survivors of sexual child abuse and those who care for them."

For Crying Out Loud 46 Pleasant St., Cambridge, MA 02139.

Survivorship – A Newsletter For Ritual Abuse Survivors 3181 Mission #139, San Francisco, CA 94110.

ORGANIZATIONS AND SUPPORT GROUPS

VOICES in Action, PO Box 148309, Chicago, IL 60614; phone: 1-800-786-4238. National network of survivors and supporters of survivors; resource material; newsletter; national and regional conferences; tapes.

Adults Molested as Children United/Parents United, c/o The Giaretto Institute, 232 E. Gish Rd., 1st Floor, San Jose, CA 95112-4703 / phone: 408-453-7616. Nationwide referrals for male and female survivors; voice mail: wait for directions to a real person and ask for a referral (9 am–5:30 pm Pacific Time).

Believe the Children, PO Box 797, Cary, IL 60013 / phone: 708-515-5432. Resources, support, public awareness on ritual and cult-related child sexual abuse.

Healing Hearts, (for ritual abuse survivors) 1515 Webster St., Oakland, CA 94612

Incest Survivors Anonymous, PO Box 17245, Long Beach, CA 90807-7245. A 12-step support group with chapters in most major cities.

Survivors of Incest Anonymous (SIA), PO Box 21817, Baltimore, MD 21222 / phone: 410-282-3400. Referrals and starter information for 12-step self-help groups for women and men over age 18. Pen-pals, bi-monthly bulletins, speakers, literature.

CATALOGS

Safer Society Press, PO Box 340, Brandon, VT 05733, phone 802-247-3132. See next page for selected titles.

Launch Press, PO Box 5629, Rockville, MD 20855, phone 1-800-321-9167.

Sidran Foundation, 2328 West Joppa Road, Suite 15, Lutherville, MD 21093, phone 410-825-8888, or e-mail sidran@access.digex.net.

Varied Directions International, 69 Elm St. Camden, ME 04843, phone 1-800-888-5236. Fax 207-236-4512. Request catalogue of audio-visual materials for survivors and clinicians.

Gift from Within, One Lily Pond Drive, Camden, ME 04843. Audio-visual materials and penpal service for people with PTSD and clinicians treating them.

SELECT SAFER SOCIETY
PUBLICATIONS

The Brother/Sister Hurt: Recognizing the Effects of Sibling Abuse by Vernon Wiehe, Ph.D. (1996). Approx. 128 pages. $10.00 A compassionate examination of childhood relationships among siblings. With testimony from among 150 sibling abuse survivors, Dr. Wiehe defines physical, emotional, and sexual sibling abuse, validates its seriousness, recognizes its long-lasting effects, and encourages the reader to move on in life by getting help with any resulting problems.

Shining Through: Pulling It Together After Sexual Abuse by Mindy Loiselle, MSW and Leslie Bailey Wright, MSW (1995). 96 pages. $12.00. Gentle, healing workbook for girls (or alters) aged 10 to 16.

Adults Molested As Children: A Survivor's Manual for Women & Men by Euan Bear with Peter Dimock (1988; 4th printing). 66 pages. $12.95. Best beginner's book on sexual abuse — good explanations of the effects of abuse for friends and family members, too.

Family Fallout: A Handbook for Families of Sexual Abuse Survivors by Dorothy Beaulieu Landry, MEd (1991). Foreword by Suzanne Sgroi, MD. 76 pages. $12.95. Validates emotional reactions of family members learning of their adult loved one's sexual abuse in childhood while guiding them toward acceptance and support.

Embodying Healing: Integrating Bodywork and Psychotherapy in Recovery from Childhood Sexual Abuse by Robert J. Timms, PhD, and Patrick Connors, CMT (1992). Foreword by Christine Courtois, PhD. 96 pages. $15.00. Provides theory, guidelines, practice notes, case histories, and most important, a thorough discussion of ethical issues involved in using bodywork with psychotherapy.

Offender-Victim Communication: A Face-to-Face Session (Video: 57 minutes). Seven sexual abusers face the camera and answer 21 questions frequently asked by survivors, asked aloud by a woman who is a survivor of sexual abuse. The answers are sometimes honest, self-centered or unconvincing, but usually illuminating. (1995). $100.

The Banner Project: Breaking the Silence of Sexual Abuse (Video: 43 minutes). Features 3 survivors of childhood sexual abuse (2 women and 1 man) talking about their experiences against the backdrop of the Banner Project, quilted panels made by hundreds of survivors (1994). Intense imagery. $40.

The Safer Society Press publishes additional books, audiocassettes, and training videos related to the treatment of sexual abuse. For a catalog of our complete listings, please check the box on the order form (next page).

BOOK ORDER FORM

Date_____

SHIPPING ADDRESS: ☐ *Please send a catalog*

Name and/or Agency_____

Address_____

City_____ State_____ Zip_____

BILLING ADDRESS *(if different from shipping address)*:

Address_____

City_____ State_____ Zip_____

Daytime Phone (_____) _____

QTY	TITLE	UNIT PRICE	TOTAL COST

		SUB TOTAL	
		VT RESIDENTS ADD SALES TAX	
		SHIPPING *(SEE BELOW)*	
		TOTAL	

Make checks payable to:
SAFER SOCIETY PRESS

*All prices subject to change
without notice.*

NO RETURNS.

Mail to:
SAFER SOCIETY PRESS
PO Box 340
Brandon, Vermont 05733-0340
(802) 247-3132

Shipping:
1-9 items add $5.00 shipping
10 or more items add 8% shipping
Bulk Order add 8%
Rush Order add $10.00